NFL★TODAY

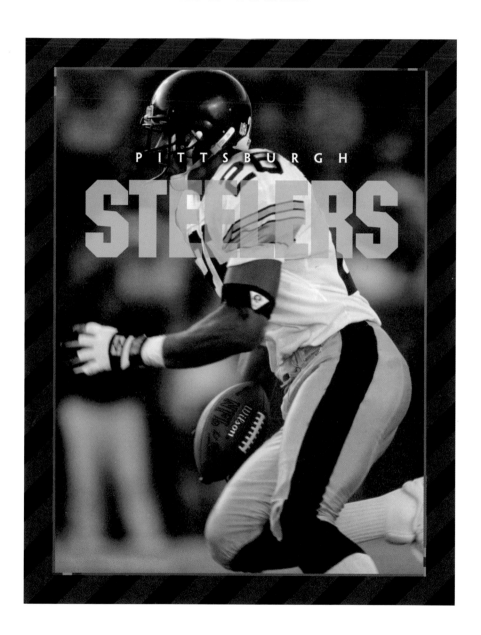

PITTSBURGH
STEELERS

MICHAEL GOODMAN

CREATIVE ⓒ EDUCATION

Published by Creative Education
123 South Broad Street, Mankato, Minnesota 56001
Creative Education is an imprint of The Creative Company

Designed by Rita Marshall
Cover illustration by Rob Day

Photos by: Allsport Photography, Associated Press,Bettmann Archive,
Focus on Sports, Fotosport, Spectra Action, and SportsChrome.

Library of Congress Cataloging-in-Publication Data

Goodman, Michael E.
Pittsburgh Steelers / by Michael Goodman.
p. cm. — (NFL Today)
Summary: Traces the history of the team from its beginnings through 1996.
ISBN 0-88682-798-1

1. Pittsburgh Steelers (Football team)—History—Juvenile literature.
[1. Pittsburgh Steelers (Football team) 2. Football—History.]
I. Title. II. Series.

GV956.P57G66   1996   96-15247
796.332'64'0974886—dc20

123456

In the early 1970s, Pittsburgh, Pennsylvania, went through
a rebirth. It came about because work was slowing down
at the local steel mills, and unemployment was high. But the
people of Pittsburgh believed that there was more to their hometown than mills, buildings and smoke. They knew that the city's
most valuable resource was the people themselves. So they
cleaned up their city and began rebuilding it. As a result,
Pittsburgh was transformed into one of America's "most liv-
able" communities.

During this same period, Pittsburgh's professional football
team, the Steelers, was undergoing a rebirth of its own. For

An early Pittsburgh star, John Henry Johnson.

·nearly 40 years, the Steelers had floundered near the bottom of the National Football League. Then, in the early 1970s, an innovative coach named Chuck Noll began reconstructing the Steelers' offense and defense around such future Hall of Famers as Terry Bradshaw, Franco Harris, Jack Lambert and Joe Greene. Noll established a new winning attitude and the Steelers rose to the top of the league, capturing four Super Bowls in the years between 1975 and 1980.

The newfound dominance of the Steelers was almost as remarkable as the turnaround of the city of Pittsburgh. It was fitting that the two success stories occurred together since hard-working fans in "the Steel City" have always closely identified with their heroes in the black-and-gold uniforms. It was also fitting that this Super Bowl contender was being led by a Pittsburgh native, head coach Bill Cowher.

1   9   3   3

Art Rooney bought the original fran-chise for $2,500 with money he won on a lucky bet at Saratoga racetrack.

ONE MAN'S DREAM

From the franchise's beginnings in the 1930s, Pittsburgh foot-ball teams were noted for their hard-nosed effort but not, unfortunately, for their ability to win. For many years the Steelers were like a dormant volcano. Smoldering and steaming, they had potential for greatness but had yet to erupt. Only one man firmly believed that the volcano would someday explode. That man was Art Rooney.

Arthur Joseph Rooney was born in 1901, the eldest of nine children. As a young man, Rooney was good enough to be signed to a baseball contract by the Boston Red Sox, but an arm injury ended his hopes of a playing career. Art was still determined to make sports his life, however, and he began exploring the idea of owning a team.

An Art Rooney favorite, L.C. Greenwood (#68) (page 7).

1 9 4 1

Poor Pittsburgh! The Steelers lost a game to Green Bay by 47 points—their worst loss ever.

Two key events happened in 1933 to help make Rooney's dream a reality. The first was the passage of a new Pennsylvania state law permitting football games to be played on Sundays. The old law had kept teams from Pittsburgh or Philadelphia out of the NFL, which scheduled Sunday games. The second event involved a lucky bet that Rooney made at the Saratoga horse-racing track in New York. With his $2,500 in winnings, the young Irishman purchased a Pittsburgh franchise in the NFL.

Rooney called his team the Pirates, after his favorite baseball team. He was certain that the sports fans in Pittsburgh would support these football Pirates, too. After all, pro football had a long history in western Pennsylvania. Forty years before Rooney fielded his team, a former Yale star named Pudge Heffelfinger had been paid $500 to play for the Allegheny Athletic Association. Pudge earned his money by causing a fumble, carrying the football across the goal line and touching it to the ground for a four-point "touchdown." The word "touchdown" was first borrowed from English rugby. In that game, the ball must be touched to the ground in the end zone for a score. Those points helped Allegheny defeat the Pittsburgh Athletic Club, 4-0, in our nation's first pro football game.

Unfortunately, Rooney's team didn't have anyone with Pudge Heffelfinger's talent. The squad of young rookies and semi-pro veterans finished the 1933 season in last place in the NFL's Eastern Division with a 3-6-2 record. If the team's play wasn't embarrassing enough, their uniforms were even worse. Rooney clad his players in striped jerseys that made them look like fugitives from a chain gang. Opposing players called them "jailbirds."

Rooney soon changed the uniforms, but he couldn't alter the

team's fortunes. The Pirates didn't record a single winning season during the 1930s.

In 1941, Rooney brought in a new coach, Bert Bell, and changed the club's nickname to the Steelers, in honor of the city's major industry. However, after watching a pre-season workout, Rooney said, "Well, we've got a new team, a new coach, a new nickname, and new uniforms, but they look like the same old Pirates to me." He was right. Pittsburgh again finished in last place with a 1-9-1 record. Rooney dismissed Bell and brought back the team's former coach, Walt Kiesling.

Kiesling directed a remarkable turnaround in 1942, leading the club to its first winning record ever at 7-4. The Steelers' star was halfback Bill Dudley, who led the NFL in rushing. The team's "winning streak" didn't last very long, however. In 1943, Dudley and several other key players left Pittsburgh to serve in World War II and the Steelers' record dipped back below .500 again.

Giant collapse! The Steelers defeated New York by 56 points—their biggest margin of victory ever.

A CHANGE OF LUCK

Walt Kiesling served three stints as coach in Pittsburgh, but few of those years were as successful as 1942. His last term, in particular, was disastrous for the Steelers' future. In 1955, Kiesling released a rookie quarterback named John Unitas during training camp. "Unitas can't remember the plays. He's too dumb," Kiesling told Rooney. Yet the Baltimore Colts decided to give Unitas a chance, and he led the Colts to three NFL championships during a long Hall-of-Fame career.

After a mistake like this, Pittsburgh's luck just had to change. In 1957, the club's fortunes did improve when Rooney picked

The highly versatile Kordell Stewart (pages 10-11).

"Big Daddy" Lipscomb was the Steelers' fiercest pass rusher.

Buddy Parker to be the Steelers' new coach. Parker, who had previously won three divisional titles with the Detroit Lions, concentrated on building an offense around quarterback Earl Morrall and receiver Jack McClairen. This talented combination led the Steelers to a 6-6 record. The next year, Parker made a big trade, obtaining Bobby Layne, who had quarterbacked Parker's best Lions squads. Layne was a flamboyant star who played hard on Sunday afternoons and partied hard the rest of the week. He was also an outstanding competitor. "I never lost a game," he once told a reporter. "I just ran out of time."

Parker also made a key trade with the San Francisco 49ers, obtaining halfback John Henry Johnson to team with Layne in the Pittsburgh backfield. Johnson rushed for more than 4,300 yards in six seasons in Pittsburgh to earn a place in the Hall of Fame. Parker's defense was led by lineman Gene "Big Daddy" Lipscomb, a one-man wrecking crew.

The Steelers, with these stars leading the way, had five records of .500 or better in eight years. In Layne's last season with the team, 1962, Pittsburgh finished at 9-5 and earned a post-season berth. The Steelers lasted only one round in the playoffs, however, falling to the Detroit Lions, 17-10, in a hard-fought battle.

Art Rooney's sleeping volcano was beginning to rumble, but it would be another ten years before it would erupt.

Rooney did his part in stirring up the volcano in 1969 when he hired Baltimore assistant Chuck Noll as the club's 14th head coach. Noll had two things going for him: his football knowledge and his patience. He felt that the best way to build the Steelers would be slowly through the NFL Draft. His first pick turned out to be one of the best in the club's history—a tall defensive lineman from North Texas State named Joe Greene. Greene's college teammates and opponents called him "Mean Joe," and his professional opponents soon learned why. "He didn't get that nickname because he liked to pick daisies," Redskins' quarterback Joe Theismann would later comment. Noll also selected a second outstanding defensive lineman in the 1969 draft, L.C. Greenwood.

Noll's patience was tested that first year, when the Steelers won their opening game and then lost 13 straight. They did score one big victory following the season, however, winning the coin toss for the right to choose first in the 1970 NFL Draft. Noll used that pick to take quarterback Terry Bradshaw of Louisiana Tech.

L.C. Greenwood recovered a record five fumbles.

Like most Southern youngsters, Terry Bradshaw began playing football at an early age. As a child, he was small and skinny, and he had to prove he was tough enough to play football. He was even cut from his junior high team. "Your time will come," Terry's father told him. "Just make sure you're ready when it does."

Bradshaw worked hard to improve his football skills and finally won the starting quarterback position on his high school team as a senior. Then he proved he was ready to be a star by throwing for over 1,400 yards and 21 touchdowns. Those statistics earned him a football scholarship to Louisiana Tech, 75 miles from his home in Shreveport.

When Bradshaw graduated four years later, the once-skinny boy had become a muscular, six-foot-three, 215-pound man, who could throw the ball 70 yards in the air. Every pro team wanted him, but Chuck Noll's Steelers got him.

When Bradshaw reported to the Steelers' rookie camp, however, he felt as awkward as he had back in junior high. He was lonely so far from home and trying too hard to do things right on the field.

In his first professional game against the Houston Oilers, Bradshaw misfired on nine straight passes and completed only four of 16 before Noll mercifully benched him. After the game Bradshaw told reporters, "The benching put a big lump in my throat. I told myself, 'What now, big shot? Everybody was counting on you, and you blew it.'"

Bradshaw began to doubt himself during that tough first year. In desperation, Bradshaw asked his college coach to send films from his college games so he could see who he really was. "I was trying to be Joe Namath or somebody, instead of being myself," he reflected. He decided to concentrate on being Terry Bradshaw.

1970

Rookie Terry Bradshaw threw more interceptions than touchdowns in his first year.

THE TEAM OF THE SEVENTIES

While Bradshaw was working through his problems, the Steelers offensive line, anchored by center Ray Mansfield and tackle Jon Kolb, was beginning to gel. Noll knew that a solid line was vital to protect his young quarterback. But what the team really needed was a strong running game to balance Bradshaw's passing. So Noll made Penn State fullback Franco Harris the Steelers' first-round draft choice in 1972.

"Franco was the key man on our ball club," noted teammate Joe Greene. "We were coming on every year in the 1970s, getting better and better. All we needed was the catalyst, and Franco was it."

After a slow start at the beginning of the 1972 season, Harris rushed for more than 100 yards in six straight games, tying what

Bradshaw led the Steelers with 212 career touchdowns.

*Joe Greene
anchored the Steel
Curtain defense.*

was then an NFL record. Led by Harris, the Steelers won nine of their last ten games to capture the AFC Central Division title and earn their first playoff berth since 1962.

Harris saved his greatest play of the 1972 season for the end of Pittsburgh's playoff game against the Oakland Raiders. With only 22 seconds to go, Oakland was leading 7-6. Things looked pretty hopeless to Steelers fans, and Art Rooney left the owner's box at Three Rivers Stadium to go down and congratulate his players on their fine season.

While he was in the elevator, Rooney could just make out the sound of the crowd roaring. He raced onto the field, where he learned about Harris' miracle play.

With the clock ticking down, Terry Bradshaw had rolled out from his 40-yard line when he spotted halfback John "Frenchy" Fuqua in the open. He rifled the ball toward Fuqua, but Raiders defensive back Jack Tatum arrived at the same time as the ball, crushing Fuqua with a ferocious hit. The ball bounced straight back toward Bradshaw like a rocket. Before it could hit the ground, however, Harris, who had been trailing the play, caught the ball near his shoe tops and outraced Oakland defenders to the end zone for the winning touchdown. Harris' remarkable catch became known as "the Immaculate Reception."

Unfortunately, not even Franco Harris could stop the Miami Dolphins express the next week. The Dolphins edged the Steelers, 21-17, in the AFC championship game on their way to an undefeated season and a Super Bowl win.

Noll's draft-pick success reached its high point in 1974, when the Pittsburgh coach selected wide receivers Lynn Swann and John Stallworth, linebacker Jack Lambert and center Mike Webster. Those players would eventually earn 24 Pro Bowl appearances and 16 Super Bowl rings.

Propelled by the success of the draft, Art Rooney's "Black-

L.C. Geenwood hunted opposing ball carriers.   17

and-Gold" captured Super Bowl IX following the 1974 season. After 41 years, the Steelers had finally brought a championship to Pittsburgh. The big star of the 16-6 Pittsburgh win over the Minnesota Vikings was Franco Harris, who rushed for a record 158 yards, but the biggest winner was Art Rooney.

"Today's win made all the other years worth it," said Rooney, his voice quivering with emotion. "I am happy for the coaches and players, but I'm especially happy for the Pittsburgh fans. They deserved this."

The Steelers didn't want to be known as one- or even two-year wonders, so they went out and captured three more Super Bowls during the next five years. They defeated the Dallas Cowboys 21-17 in Super Bowl X and 35-31 in Super Bowl XIII and then crushed the Los Angeles Rams 31-19 in Super Bowl XIV. Those victories earned the Steelers the title "the Team of the Seventies."

Throughout the club's championship years, the cast remained basically the same. Terry Bradshaw, Franco Harris, and Rocky Bleier starred in the backfield; wide receivers Lynn Swann and John Stallworth made acrobatic receptions; and Jack Lambert, Jack Ham, Andy Russell, Mel Blount, Donnie Shell, Joe Greene and L.C. Greenwood dominated on an impenetrable defense known as "the Steel Curtain."

1 9 7 4

Jack Lambert began his climb to membership in the Hall of Fame.

UP AND DOWN IN THE '80S

As the Steelers entered the 1980s, the greats retired one by one. Chuck Noll tried to rebuild by drafting young stars such as Greg Hawthorne, Frank Pollard and Mark Malone on offense and Robin Cole, Mike Merriweather and Dennis Winston on defense. These new team leaders helped the Steelers maintain their winning ways.

In 1983 and 1984, Pittsburgh captured AFC Central Division titles for the eighth and ninth times in 13 seasons. In the 1983 playoffs, they were defeated handily, 38-10, by the Los Angeles Raiders. However, things looked brighter in 1984. Led by Malone, Pollard and outstanding rookie receiver Louis Lipps, the Steelers edged out Denver, 24-17, to reach the AFC championship game against the Miami Dolphins. The new Steelers came up short in that contest, but the 45-28 loss didn't worry Art Rooney. "This is an upbeat team," he said. "There is so much youth, so much hope for the future."

1 9 8 8

Frank Pollard carried the ball in the '80s more than any other Steeler.

But the Steelers' good fortunes did not continue. The club failed to make the playoffs for four straight years between 1985 and 1988. The two bright spots during those years were the play of Lipps at wide receiver and Rod Woodson at defensive back. But Art Rooney knew that the Steelers could still win with the right talent, particularly the right quarterback.

To find their new field general, Rooney and Noll looked once again to Louisiana. Walter Andrew Brister III, known to his friends as "Bubby," was a standout quarterback at Northeast Louisiana University. The Steelers made Brister their third pick in the 1986 draft.

Bubby took a while to get his bearings in the NFL, but he finally made his mark in a game against Houston late in the 1988 season. He tossed three touchdown passes, including the game-winner to running back Merril Hoge with just 20 seconds left, to spearhead a 37-34 upset of the Oilers.

Houston coach Jerry Glanville was impressed with Brister. "We put some hellacious hits on the kid and he kept ticking,"

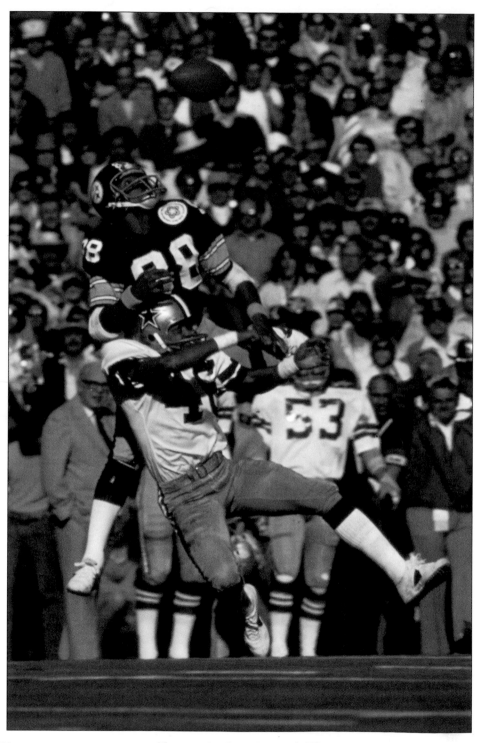

The amazing Lynn Swann (#88).

he remarked. "This guy is a competitor. If he wasn't playing quarterback, he'd be starting at free safety and punching people in the mouth."

From this performance Brister's confidence grew and grew. At the spring minicamp in 1989, Bubby wrote the words "PLAY-OFFS 89" on a chalkboard. Then he went out to make his prediction come true. The Steelers won five of their final six games to return to the playoffs. Then, in a first-round game against Houston, Brister engineered another last-second drive to tie the contest and send it into overtime. A few minutes later, Gary Anderson's 50-yard field goal won the game, 26-23.

A narrow loss to Denver the following week ended Brister's storybook season, but Steelers fans were certain that better times were ahead in the 1990s. Unfortunately, Art Rooney would not be around to see them. The father of professional football in Pittsburgh for more than 55 years died just prior to the 1989 season.

Battering running back Barry Foster averaged 5.1 yards per carry for the Steelers.

A RESURGENT DECADE

The new decade saw lots of changes for the Black-and-Gold, including several bright new stars. In some of his important moves before retiring after the 1991 season, Chuck Noll drafted quarterback Neil O'Donnell from Maryland, huge tight end Eric Green from Liberty, and explosive halfback Barry Foster from Arkansas to take over Pittsburgh's offense. O'Donnell began the 1991 season sharing the signal-calling duties with Bubby Brister, but soon won the starting role because of his more accurate throwing arm and greater ability to scramble out of trouble. Noll also left the defense in good hands with young stars such as Rod Woodson, already rated one of the best defensive backs of all time, and linebacker Greg Lloyd.

Left to right: Neal O'Donnell, Rod Woodson, Jack Lambert, Franco Harris.

Noll brought these men to Pittsburgh, but it was up to Pittsburgh native Bill Cowher, who took over the coaching reins in 1992, to mold them into a winning team. Cowher, a former NFL linebacker and defensive assistant coach, realized he was on the "hot seat" when he replaced a legend like Noll, but it was a job he had been waiting for all of his life. Growing up not far from Three Rivers Stadium, he had been a Steelers fan. "I still remember registering him for Pop Warner football," said Cowher's father Laird. "Now that same boy is back home coaching the hometown team I've lived and died for my whole life. What a fairy tale."

Defensive star Rod Woodson also led the team in punt and kick returns.

Fairy tale or not, what Cowher achieved in his first year at the helm was magical. The team went 11-5, capturing another Central Division title, Neil O'Donnell completed nearly 60 percent of his passes for over 2,200 yards, Barry Foster led the AFC in rushing with a team record 1,690 yards and Cowher was named NFL Coach of the Year. Not bad for a rookie!

The Steelers made the playoffs again in 1993 and 1994, using brute force on both offense and defense, much like those "volcanic" Pittsburgh teams of the 1970s. The club's play prompted media headlines such as "Back to the Future" and "Hard Hats Again."

The Steelers wanted badly to get back to another Super Bowl, and they came within inches of doing so in 1994. After a season in which they had led the AFC with a 12-4 record and all NFL clubs with 55 sacks, the Steelers were confident of their ability to earn a place in Super Bowl XXIX in Miami. Pittsburgh romped over Cleveland 29-9 in the first round of the playoffs and were clear favorites against the San Diego Chargers in the AFC title game at home the following week. However, San Diego

Formerly unsung, Ernie Mills is now a dynamic receiver (pages 26-27).

Head coach Bill Cowher established himself as one of the premier motivators in the NFL.

scored two second-half touchdowns to take a 17-13 lead with just over five minutes remaining. Then Chargers defenders held off a desperate Pittsburgh comeback, breaking up a potential touchdown pass from O'Donnell to Barry Foster in the closing seconds to win the game and the conference title.

The Steelers' motto for the 1995 season became "Three More Yards." That was how much farther the Pittsburgh offense needed to have gone to score the winning touchdown against San Diego and make it to the Super Bowl the year before. The team covered that distance and more during the 1995 campaign, finishing atop the AFC Central once again with an 11-5 record and then defeating the Buffalo Bills and Indianapolis Colts to earn an opportunity to return to the Super Bowl for the first time in 16 years.

Three young "veterans" emerged on offense during 1995—running back Erric Pegram and wide receiver Ernie Mills, signed as free agents before the season began, and receiver Yancey Thigpen, whose 85 catches during the year set a new club record. But the player who created the most excitement was rookie Kordell Stewart from Colorado. Stewart was drafted as a quarterback, but soon began practicing at other offensive positions as well. Coach Cowher gave him the nickname "Slash," because his position in the team program was listed as "quarterback-slash(/)-running back-slash(/)-wide receiver." Cowher also designed new plays to take advantage of "Slash's" versatility. During one series in a late-season game, Stewart, as quarterback, tossed a pair of passes to Thigpen and Mills, then lined up at wide receiver, took a pitch out from O'Donnell and raced 22 yards for a touchdown.

Stewart's multiple roles gave him a unique perspective on the passing game. "I've got a lot of confidence when Slash is

Kevin Green was a top sack threat in the 1990s.

Running back Jerome Bettis provides veteran leadership for the Steelers.

in there passing that he won't throw the ball too high so that a receiver is stretched out and can get hurt," said Mills. "He knows how he'd feel if the positions were reversed."

The new offensive stars, plus the continued fine play of defensive leaders Greg Lloyd, Kevin Greene and Levon Kirkland, helped the Steelers reach Super Bowl XXX but couldn't lead the team to victory over the Dallas Cowboys in the championship game. The hard-fought contest ended with Dallas on top, 27-17, but the game was really closer than that. Two misguided O'Donnell passes that wound up in the hands of Cowboys defender Larry Brown halted Steelers drives that could have won the game for Pittsburgh.

But Bill Cowher is not spending his time thinking about what might have been; he's concentrating on the future. He believes the nucleus is in place for another Pittsburgh NFL dynasty. That loud rumbling football fans around the country hear just might be another championship volcano erupting in the Steel City.